PARAÍSO

CANTO MUNDO

POETRY SERIES

EDITED BY DEBORAH PAREDEZ
AND CELESTE MENDOZA

PARAÍSO

POEMS BY JACOB SHORES-ARGÜELLO

The University of Arkansas Press
Fayetteville
2017

ISBN: 978-1-68226-043-2
e-ISBN: 978-1-61075-620-4

21 20 19 18 17   5 4 3 2 1

Designed by Liz Lester

♾ The paper used in this publication meets the minimum
requirements of the American National Standard for Permanence
of Paper for Printed Library Materials Z39.48-1984.

Library of Congress Control Number: 2017941840

In memory of my mother,
Flor Shores-Argüello

SERIES EDITORS' PREFACE

"Everything," Jacob Shores-Argüello writes, "is not / perfect, but everything is prayer." In these lines and everywhere in his poetry, he conveys a reverence for the wounded and for the pilgrimages we undertake in search of healing. His poems observe and enact the rites, ruminations, and diversions we invent as guides through the landscapes of grief and recovery. From a bus's "skipped-piston rhythm" along Costa Rica's mountainside to a hospital bedside vigil, from the streets of Oklahoma to the "jungle's thin stabs of sun," these poems migrate across linguistic and geographical borders in ways that resonate with the long tradition of Latina/o poetics. And in the self-implicating and multivocal registers in which his work speaks—lyric, imperative, dialogic—Shores-Argüello simultaneously forges new pathways for the future of Latina/o poetry. In this way, *Paraíso* is an especially fitting recipient of the inaugural CantoMundo Poetry Prize.

Since our founding in 2009 by a collective of cross generational Latina/o poets—Norma E. Cantú, Celeste Guzman Mendoza, Pablo Miguel Martínez, Deborah Paredez, and Carmen Tafolla—CantoMundo has sought to provide a space for the creation of Latina/o poetry and a community of support for Latina/o poets. Our vision and our methods have been undeniably shaped by the transformative work of poets of color who organized the Floricanto gatherings during the social and artistic movements of the 1960s and 1970s and those who founded Cave Canem in the 1990s and Kundiman in the early 2000s. Central to CantoMundo's mission is the desire to create opportunities—both within and beyond established institutions—for the development, documentation, performance, and publication of Latina/o poetry. A *canto-mundo*, a world of song, sustained by the wide-ranging voices of Latina/o poets.

The CantoMundo Poetry Series is an extension of CantoMundo's efforts to support and showcase Latina/o poets from across the linguistic, aesthetic, stylistic, and cultural spectrums in which they write. The series values the traditions and communities from which contemporary Latina/o poets emerge while also encouraging an engagement with innovative Latina/o aesthetics and poetics. To this end, we invited Aracelis Girmay to act as our inaugural judge because of the ways her work has both embodied and transformed Latina/o poetry's particular entanglements with language. Girmay observes, "I write these poems in English wishing I could write my way out of it," and in this way she captures a guiding aesthetic principle for many Latina/o poets. Shores-Argüello shares with Girmay an engagement with elegy's summoning of presence and absence and an enactment of connection across the Latina/o diaspora. The work of both poets evocatively reveals language's power to reanimate the lost while also performing language's limits in facilitating reunion and repair. About *Paraíso*, Girmay observes:

> From the opening page of Jacob Shores-Argüello's *Paraíso*, I noticed how honed and pared his work is. He is a craftsman. His poems are chiseled, sculptural even, and yet they seem to ring an ethereal ring, like glass under a finger. These are poems filled with the surprise and humility of traversing physical geographies (mountains and jungles), but also the geographies of grief, healing, and memory. I am deeply moved by their vulnerability and unending quest for closeness.

This desire for and demonstration of connection permeates *Paraíso* with its focus on the congregational spaces of bus rides and healing rituals and funeral rites and child-hood mischief, and is perhaps most powerfully conveyed in "Games," the book's formally daring first section, in which the speaker describes a series of games invented to traverse the distances across grief and isolation: "There is no winner. You just go back and forth. It is only for playing, for being together." Here, then, is the summoning of a dwelling place for our anguish and our attempts to reach beyond it toward one another. In *Paraíso*, Shores-Argüello offers us not simply a chronicle but a manual, a hymnal even, of the "many songs of devotion. Many songs / of devotion undone."

Deborah Paredez
Celeste Mendoza

ACKNOWLEDGMENTS

Thank you to the editors of the following journals where these poems, sometimes in different forms, first appeared: *Poetry*: "Pilgrims," "Reception;" *The Journal*: "Pura Vida;" *Paris American*: "Walking Tree," "Truth Potion;" *Cutthroat*: "Joke, Fact, Anecdote," "Pantone 292," "Ten Times," "A Howling Game; *The Oxford American*: "Ghost Story."

I am deeply grateful to those individuals and institutions who made this book possible: CantoMundo, the Amy Clampitt Residency Program, the Djerassi Resident Artists Program, the Fine Arts Work Center in Provincetown, Dzanc Books DISQUIET International Literary Program, Texas Tech University, Mary Angelino, Michael Argüello Barquero, Gustavo Chaves, Robin Getzen, Aracelis Girmay, Rebecca Gayle Howell, Jill Paterson, John Poch, Michael Shewmaker, Carmen Giménez Smith, Marcus Wicker, and Vicente Yépez.

And to Chloe Honum, with love.

CONTENTS

IV MAGICAL-RATIONALISM

I

GAMES

1. Joke, Fact, Anecdote

For this game you need at least three people.

One of you names a category (anything you'd like), and it is up to you to claim a **Joke**, **Fact**, or **Anecdote** for that category. For instance, if someone else calls **Fact**, then you are stuck with choosing between **Joke** or **Anecdote**. Choose quickly or you'll be stuck with **Joke**. Everyone wants anecdote. People always want to talk about their own life, even if it's a game.

> **Example Category: Elephants**
>
> Player 1 has called **Anecdote:**
>> *I got separated from my mom at a circus when I was a kid. The animal handler had me feed lettuce to the elephant to calm me down.*
>
> Player 2 has called **Joke:**
>> *Why did the elephant like rum?*
>> *He drank to forget.*
>
> Player 3 has called **Fact:**
>> *They have funerals. When one of them dies they huddle in a circle. They pass the bones from trunk to trunk.*

You agree on which of the three tries was best. Then the winner picks the next category.

I play a lot of games. Games that I have made up, games to play with the person next to me on a long plane or bus ride.

I have spent half my life growing up in the United States—
Florida, Texas, Oklahoma—the other half in my mother's
home country of Costa Rica. That's a lot of back and forth.
People have been left behind. People have left me behind.

I've been told that I like games because I am an only child.
People say that only children try to convince the world to
play with them so they're no longer alone. But it's more
than that. My Oklahoma uncle says he feels sorry for me.
His idea is that I am half Costa Rican and half not, that I
wouldn't know where to run when shit goes down. I think
that's the reason I like to play games. It's important to make
little connections with anyone you can.

You don't need anything special for these games—no cards,
dice, or paper. All you need is someone to play with. Play
them separately. Play them all at once.

2. Pantone 292

The game Pantone 292 is named after a lyric in a song in which the singer talks about how blue she feels after someone important has left her. She tells you exactly what shade of blue she is: Pantone 292.

So, the game is to pick a color (it doesn't have to be blue) and then go through the alphabet. With every letter, you are required to pick a good way to describe that color. Apple *Red* wouldn't work. Not interesting enough. Artery *Red* is a little better.

It can be a short phrase, too: **B**aboon Ass *Red*. You can play this with as many people as you want. There is no winner. You just go back and forth. It is only for playing, for being together.

Lets pick *Blue*:

American flag *Blue*
Blood in the veins *Blue*
Costa Rican flag *Blue*
Dandruff shampoo *Blue*
Earth as seen from space *Blue*
Flame-base *Blue*
Gunmetal *Blue*

And so on.

Now that I am thinking about it, I guess my mother was where I'd go when "shit went down." The kids in the streets of Oklahoma did not want me. The kids in the streets of Costa Rica did not want me. The country I had was her.

Example **Anecdote** if the category is **Mothers:**

She had stomach cancer. Not for long, though; you can't have it for too long. Sometimes the nurses didn't let me in to see her. They thought I was in the wrong hospital. Maybe I should try Hospital La Catolica in San José, where the American retirees can afford to die.

Example **Joke** if the category is **Nurses:**

A nurse reaches for the pen in her purse to sign a check but instead pulls out a rectal thermometer. *Damn,* she says, *some asshole's got my pen.*

3. Ten Times

You play Ten Times by counting down from ten to one. In each round, you have to say something you have done exactly that many times in your life. Alternate back and forth. It is a good way to get to know a person quickly.

10 Times in My Life:
I have swum in a river naked.

9 Times in My Life:
I have slept in an airport.

8 Times in My I Life:
I have ducked from the sound of a shotgun blast.

7 Times in My Life:
I have kissed a person I did not know.

And so on.

Hospital scrub *Blue*
I.V. *Blue*
Jesusy *Blue*
Knife steel *Blue*
Loneliness *Blue*
Moon in song lyric *Blue*
Nothing left to believe in *Blue*

Example **Anecdote** if the category is **Belief:**

My grandfather grew up in an adobe house. He said it was good luck to keep a coin in a hole under your bed. That was the worst thing when everybody stopped living in adobe— the dirt floors got replaced with concrete. No more holes to put coins in. No more luck.

He said that a witch had told him to do this, or a spirit. Maybe it was the rat-tailed beast that would walk with him to school; it slithered along the coffee plantation's barbed wire. The details changed, but the coin always stayed the same.

> **6 Times in My Life:**
> I have watched an erupting volcano.
>
> **5 Times in My Life:**
> I have told a story that made a small child cry.
>
> **4 Times in My Life:**
> I have gotten lost walking in a cloud.
>
> **3 Times in My Life:**
> I have been pulled out by riptide.
>
> **2 Times in My Life:**
> I have spoken at the head of a church.

Ocean *Blue*

Park Place on a Monopoly board *Blue*

Quetzal *Blue*

Example **Anecdote** if the category is **Monopoly:**

The town in Costa Rica where my family comes from is famous for its witch stories. On the Costa Rican version of the Monopoly board there is a silhouette of a witch on the square where my house would be.

4. A Howling Game

Example **Anecdote** if the category is **the Supernatural:**

When my mother was on her deathbed, she wanted to hear my grandfather's ghost stories over and over again. The stories were small proofs of the afterlife. If my grandfather's spirits could live on, maybe she could, too. Believing was the best thing she had.

> **R**ed holding its breath *Blue*
> **S**anta María *Blue*
> **T**attoo *Blue*
> **U**nder the ocean *Blue*
> **V**ena basílica *Blue*
> **W**ithout you *Blue*

Example **Anecdote** if the category is **Games:**

After my mother died, my words broke. I went up to the small farm in Santa Clara that she'd left me in her will. It was a few acres of cloud forest. Because I was alone, I drank too much rum. Because I was alone, I was haunted by the howling of coyotes. I tracked them down. I made them play a new game with me, a howling game. It was called **Who Can Wake the Spirits First.**

Xanax *Blue*
Yesterday *Blue*
Zero degrees *Blue*

1 Time in My Life:
I have placed a coin
under the foot of a hospital bed.

II

CONGREGATION

Dove

A metal-throated hummingbird
tucks through a crack in the bus window.
We duck and dodge, rough our hands
through our clothes when we feel him.
We watch as he murmurs through the air,
but we don't yet love the beautiful bird.
It's only when the animal flies into Lucite,
and falls like a bullet casing onto the floor
that we claim him as our beloved thing.
A woman kneels to cup our bird, and we hold
our breath when his wings begin to blur.
It's natural to love impossible things.
The bird swoops and flutters, hovers
like the Holy Spirit above our heads.

"Dependiendo Del Tráfico"
Es El Nuevo "Si Dios Quiere"

We idle as the parade passes.
The bus's skipped-piston rhythm
spooks the horses and children.
The driver yells at the ponies dancing
in their Easter masks, at the swaying
smoke-handed priests. The bus driver
turns, shouts that we should stay
in our seats. But this is the heart
of our once-rural country, and we
want to be in a crowd of us. We step off,
eat coconut-latticed caramels
with the children. Dance the old dances,
bounce in the inflatable church.

Más Tico Que El Gallo Pinto

We drive through the fruiting season.
When the bus stops, we bend branches
through our windows and steal níspero,
water apple, giant milk-hearted guanábana.
We lean out so children can sell us empanadas
de chiverre, green mango with lime.
In the jungle, heavy birds reply to one another
with the glassy instruments of their throats.
We feel chosen because we have so much.
But when we stop to pick up a load of tourists,
we are stunned to find they know our secrets
of plenty, when they pull threads of honey
from our mountain-clung flowers.

Cerro de la Muerte

The North Americans on the bus
are frightened by our grease and gluttony:
butter-slathered hunks of chicken,
coconut cajeta, bright red jelly
that we suckle from the corners of bags.
They don't know that we're traveling
through the mountains of the dead.
We must eat fat, drink deep, and wrap
our bodies so we're not lost to the cold.
True, it's been forty years since a soul
has frozen from the unholy altitude,
but there's always another kind of dying
and we do as we've always done. Chifrijo,
flutes of fried dough, slugs of sinless rum.

Cloud Forest

Drops condense, roll across
the bus windows. Not rain, not fog;
we're in the middle of a cloud.
As the bus climbs, the motor clicks
and strains. Soon we shiver, cough
as the ice-lined cloud settles into
our lungs. We fear the mountain's cold,
and it takes so little time to make a church,
so we become chorus, sing the bus
into moving. We clap our forty hands,
drum our forty feet. We begin to believe
in the idea of us, in the frost-touched
revolutions of our impossible machine.

Faith

The bus climbs up the toothy mountain
until we're blinded by the clouds.
Our hearts jump when the busman speeds,
tempts the drop that threatens our left.
We passengers pray for the driver to stop,
give thanks when we touch bumpers
with an ambulance and are forced to slow.
Having no sympathy for emergency,
the driver yells back that we should have faith—
he could drive this route without his hands.
It's too easy to trust a man whose face
you cannot see. We gasp—but say nothing
when the driver gives the bus gas and begins
to pass the ambulance on the left-hand side.

Holy Mysteries

The bus clatters over a wood-trussed bridge.
Below, there is river-clogging brush,
tires caught in shallows, a swarm of blue
plastic bags that gives shape to the current.
We know that mosquitos breed in the holds
of old tires, and that the blue bags
carry poison for bananas. In the bus, a boy
pivots on crutches, walks the aisle with his story,
sells us plastic pens and saint-brightened cards.
At the stop, the boy springs off, gives a fold
of bills to a pock-ravaged man. We can't see
what mysteries the young boy receives.
There's only so much a passenger can know.

Pilgrims

The bus arrives in the orchid heat,
in the place where coffee grows
like rubies from the valley's black soil.
We disembark, walk in twos so we
don't slip on the biblical mud.
The woman next to me carries
three cell phones as gifts for cousins
and a bucket of chicken to share.
How is it that I have come this far
with nothing, that I am empty-
handed in this country of blessings?
A procession of rust-colored macaws
glides above us. Their ashy shadows
draw crosses onto all of our heads.

III

FUNERAL RITES

Elegy for My Mother

As a child I vandalized my grandfather
with questions, asked about the long whips

left by river snakes in the mud,
the sudden bones of birds on the jungle floor.

I cared so much about what was left behind.
Now, we are selling her last calf

because we can no longer take care of both
her animals and her land.

My grandfather smiled at the funeral,
joked that the little plot next to hers

would surely be his. Now he is serious.
We are walking the green of my mother's farm,

and he shows me again how to carry
the calf on my shoulders,

so I don't disturb her,
so I don't cause her pain.

Fire Song

The wildfire happens
         quickly. Direwinds
     huff their enormous lungs.

The vaqueros watch
     as the grasses blush
  with flame,
    and the throngs
of Brahmans stampede.

Yellowbriar, devil's ear,
   jaragua grass–
     all belong solely
  to this fire.

Without trees,
   there is entirely   too much sky.

Low low, says the tapir
   as it runs from heat. *Ruin*,
warns a swoop
    of hummingbirds.

The hot-breathed wind hisses
Who Who
     as it spits and spins.

        I look out over the fire line
and repeat my mother's name.

Many songs of devotion. Many songs
    of devotion
        undone.

Medicine

My uncle could not find the witch
but the witch's sister gave him a mash

of sweet herbs for me to drink.
I drank, but did not remember

that I drank. I drank again,
and each time I lost another day.

Until all I could remember
was walking with my mother

in the wild green of Santa Clara,
rope sawing into my shoulder,

a plastic jug of water tied at the end.
We plucked purple sage that day,

smoked ourselves, prayed. Prepared
our bodies for all that would come.

Ghost Story

As a boy I pleaded
with the river to teach me
its long and winding vowels.
In exchange I taught it
swear words, how to play games.
The night I stayed by its side
for hours, eight parrots
came to listen to us speak.
It was a long time before
the river asked in a low voice
if the children of the pueblo
had finally forgotten La Llorona—
the woman who drowned
her children in its deep waters.
Yes, I said. *Forgotten.*
It's hard to lie to a river,
harder to lie to a river you love.

Make Believe

As children, my cousin and I once
dug into the side of our mountain,

a terrible brown work.
That morning we'd made the cold walk

to the hospital and watched
his mother for a long time.

She was unchained from her machines,
shrinking into ordinary.

It was our first death,
and we looked at our small hands.

But *no*, my cousin insisted,
these are not our hands,

they are bear hands.
And we walked to our mountain,

shaped our cave:
one meter, two meters, three.

We bears were making a home.
We roared, and shook off our human bones,

until angels howled like dogs
in the valley below.

Paloma

Primo, our childhood was river weeds
twisted into crucifixes,

El Chavo del Ocho on our old TV,
and grandmother's parrot asking for coffee.

Primo, why is it so hard to talk to anyone
whose mother hasn't died?

Come to my house tomorrow
and we'll drink beer poisoned by lime,

we'll lure a moth with our flashlights
and not be ashamed to see death in everything.

We'll unfold it with our hands, Primo,
look into the eyes of its camouflaged wings.

Pura Vida

The workers broke song,
then bent to collect the last of the coffee.

Their baskets lined the shore,
notches on the river's spine.

El patrón knew my grandmother's basket
by the size of her pick. Her haul

shamed the leather-handed men.
The story goes that my grandmother

said nothing during this time of her life.
Later, after leaving behind the fields,

she loves to talk and joke.
There is only so much a spirit can do,

she says, as my cousin and I open
cashew fruit for her. She laughs at how

the curled little fruit looks like a baby's penis,
laughs with everything but her hands.

Mucho Brete, Gracias a Dios

It is very early, and dead leaves
have collected on the loading dock,

swirl when trucks arrive one by one.
My uncle drinks orange soda

through a candy-striped straw.
He's done this job for fifteen years

and is ready when the conveyor begins.
Work can be medicine, he says,

as I hook my thumbs into the webbing
of a borrowed lift belt.

When the crates come we stack them
three deep onto the dollies.

And I am happy enough,
thinking of the small things:

The cigarette butts at my feet,
the low outbound moon.

Bucolic

Slipping gears and throwing rocks,
it takes so little time before

the Jeep skids, and I am sliding
sideways into the tree line.

When I wake, eleven oatmeal-
colored calves have come to me.

They have saucer eyes, cavernous nostrils;
they make gentle tearing noises

as they strip the bushes of their leaves.
I bleed a little, but am not hurt.

I ask the calves how they have found me.
I listen to them eat and eat.

Everything is not
perfect, but everything is prayer.

After the Funeral We Go into the City

My cousin guides me through smoke-
stained doors and buys thin casino cigars

that push us into fits of coughing.
We've forgotten the games

and make wagers we don't understand,
argue with bouncers when we lose.

Wandering the city, starting fights
with men over the price of papaya,

we share rum that we carry in a bottle of Coke.
My cousin offers a swig to everyone

we pass on the street, calls them *hijo
de puta* when they don't drink.

We believe that men need excuses for pain,
that grief is a thing that bleeds.

But we are too loved to be hurt by our smog-
blessed city, and we're ashamed when we go unscathed.

In the park, a drug dealer stands in the shadow
of a fig tree, makes kissing noises to his beautiful dog.

Paraíso

We escape with Guatemalan rum
through the city's petroleum night,

through rain-washed asphalt
and taxi smog, up the volcanic hills

of San José, through neighborhoods
roofed by zinc, and fincas where

shade trees stand watch over coffee,
up the mountain's lava-made trail,

into the theater of the sky
where we can see the naked body

of the city, and higher to where
we point to our far pueblo,

and to the ocean eating up the coast,
and higher into the cold

until we can hold all of Costa Rica
in our eye, and then higher

until Mexico bulges into the ocean—
up and up until we stare out at the mingling

Americas, Florida kissing Cuba
in the blue distance, and we open our rum

and drink so long that we forget ourselves,
and remember ourselves again.

IV

MAGICAL-RATIONALISM

Cure #1: Communication with the Dead

Take your saw into the cloud forest. Look for the smooth branches of a sap-heavy tree. Cut fourteen gashes into them, sweet blood will come. Say her name.

In six days, return. Search for the cut that has attracted ants of two different species. They will be joined by hardening sap. Take this branch and only this branch. Say her name. Cut the branch down to a centimeter-long piece, the scar in the exact middle.

Split the branch at its scar with a knife. Say her name. Separate into disks, hold them up and look into these wooden eyes. Tell these eyes how you miss them. Tell these eyes not to blink.

Say her name, say her name.

Walking Tree

The squat palm is a mess of thin
root-like branches, a thousand legs
looking for sun. It leans toward
the jungle's edge, fumbling for
the ocean's empty promise of light.
The biologist tells the tourists
it has walked ten meters in twenty years.
Later, in the heat of her tent, I ask
if it's true, can a tree really escape
from its gloom-roofed life? She smiles
and says it's a balm for people who've walked
too far in the jungle's unexpected dark,
a story that tour guides and witches tell.

Transubstantiation

The ground trees practice their low
geometry. They are sideways growers,
a collapse of abstract branches
throwing their leaves far from the trunk.
All this because they're starved for sun.
But there is miracle in their chlorophyll,
the green ritual that makes life from
the heart of a star—and I am hungry.
I twist their sluicing fruits from the stem,
greedy for my portion of light. As I eat,
blood-colored juice falls to the ground.
It hurts me that the canopy shades
these trees from God. I spit their seeds
into the jungle's thin stabs of sun.

Magical-Rationalism

The rum is strong, so I don't know
if I'm flirting with the cloud forest biologist

when I tell her that we aren't so different.
The heavy glasses are cold rituals in our hands,

and I'm surprised when she doesn't go back
to her tent. She tells me that she believes

science is life and life is God.
Humans go wrong when they think only in twos.

She tells me she's writing a paper called
Hermaphrodism in the Agalychnis Callidryas,

and that's when I know for sure we're not flirting.
But I am wrong. She takes my hand and explains

it to me gently: We live in the permeable
skin of an amphibian, all the world's a frog.

Looking for Signal

I finally find the witch. She is branch-
boned, old, with knowing fingers.
She says nothing. Walks me to a tall tree,
a gourd hanging from a long line of jute.
She pulls out a phone, asks me to type
a note to my family. I do it, but can't see
how a message can be sent from somewhere
so deep. She scolds me, says that only
tourists think the world can be escaped.
The jungle's green is the wild mind
of God. The witch puts the phone into
the gourd. Hand-over-hand, she hoists
this cradle to the top of our holy canopy.

Truth Serum

The witch walks me through ferns
and twisted trunks. She plucks tongues
of leaves, handfuls of reddish petals.
She says that it's a sick thing to keep
secrets, and has me chew the perfumed
leaves of truth. Suddenly I am
speaking fast, about my mother's death,
about the shaggy wolf called grief.
Finally the witch quiets me, presses her
lips to mine—a suction kiss that draws
the serum into her mouth. She says quickly
that she's sorry. She cannot be my mother
and has no idea if I can be healed.

Medicine for Cough and Other Ills

I insist on learning the selva's
medicine. The witch takes mallow,
soaks it in lukewarm water until
it pulls into honey-thick streams.
In another pot, she boils hot pepper
in salted water, asks me to gargle and spit.
When my throat burns, she tips
the soothing cup of mallow to my lips.
Medicine is balance, she says.
I hold my hot tea with two hands,
say that I've already learned this truth.
Are you sure, the witch asks,
Rum, grief, food, sex, belief—which
of these medicines have you not abused?

Cure #2: Pain

Ingredients: A dram equal of tincture of coffee berry and epená. A red cock's comb. Two ounces of good clear rum.

Boil down cock's comb. Mix in coffee berry, add the epená. Take this essence and rub into your temples. Close your eyes, and soon the air will grow heavy with dirt. You will see the dead you always carry with you.

Ask your paradise-tied dead to stand in between you and your pain. Remember, you must remind them what hurt is. Grief is a medicine that the dead don't need. Speak slowly to them. Throw away the rum.

Arte de Sobar Pegas

The witch says she is not
a witch. She is a sobadora,

a healer who moves pain
with her hands.

Tonto, she says laughing,
and asks Mary to bless my capacity

to believe. *But why does
the pueblo call you a witch,* I ask.

She answers by taking my arm,
rubbing in long, twisting strokes

from bicep to wrist. Her hands
take away the worst part of me.

They turn to ocean on my skin,
then animals, then glossy green leaves.

Cure #3: Deciding to Leave

Take two candles still joined at the wick. They must be made of beeswax; they must be longer than your longest finger. Take star anise. Muddle with guaro or another clear spirit.

Hang your candles by a nail onto a strong-smelling níspero tree. Make sure that it is planted at the intersection of two roads, or any other place that spirits are known to gather. Drink your drink. Burn your wick.

If the candles fall into the shape of a cross, you stay. If the candles point in the same direction, go in that direction.

If the candles point to opposite places, this means nothing. It is recommended, in this case, to go anyway. If you have followed all these steps, it's because you want to go. Take your candles.

Leaf-Cutter

I scramble out of the cloud forest,
down the sheer face of a cliff,
and gash my leg on a serrated rock.
The blood is stubborn, refuses to be
quieted by pressure, by my pleading
for it to stop. Gathering a handful
of leaf-cutter ants, I place them
onto the cut, trick them into cinching
my wound shut with their mechanical bite.
The heat of their jaws reminds me
that pain is medicine. I twist their bodies
from their iron heads until I am ant-
studded, sutured. Impossibly cured.

Cure #4: For Grief

There are shape-based medicines: drink the tea of heart-shaped fruit for the pains of love. Beans for the kidney. Red tongues of leaves to bring the soothing medicine of truth.

But what is the shape of grief? Go into the wild. Think about the seat of your pain. Is it in your eye, your mouth, your body, your brain? Walk, gather your plants.

Go home. Fix your tea. It is not important that you have picked your plants correctly. It is important that you have walked. It is important that you sit and drink. That you believed.